INDIAN TRAINS

INDIAN TRAINS

Erika T. Wurth

West End Press

Poems from *Indian Trains* have been published in *Boulevard.*

First edition, November 2007
Paperback 978-0-9753486-7-3

Book and cover design by Nancy Woodard
Cover photograph by Richard Bauer
Author photograph by Craig Finlay

For book information, see our web site at www.westendpress.org

West End Press • P.O. Box 27334 • Albuquerque, N.M. 87125

CONTENTS

Indian Trains

Tracks

For My Mother & Sister

. . . Honey. The Gods are laughing at us.

—Langston Hughes

Miracles

Anger x Imagination = Survival
—Sherman Alexie

GRANDMA WAS A BEAT POET

Grandmother
was an Indian beat
poet

her daddy worked on the railroad

yes that same railroad
that beat his city Indian heart to death

and as his daughter's hands worked in the factory
he watched as one single gear
took one single finger
down the same path he had run

as his mother worked on a revolution.

STRETCHING INTO ME

I

It's 1947 and he has them all in the closet. He will punish his mother
who left him alone, who he worships above all other. Mother,

Whose arranged marriage at 15 left him for dead. Drunk, his father walked up those old
porch steps and kicked her in the stomach. She left and went home to Grandmother.

Annie James: traditional whorehouse woman, who worshiped Mary, Yussun and
the American dollar equally. She was a woman who owned her own heart,

But she could never understand her granddaughter's urge for a different kind of drum.
Grandmother sang the blues, her voice low and speaking to all of America's sides.

My Uncle Jack was her first, born with a dent in his head and a knife in his heart.
He sits in the closet with all of the others, forcing them to smoke, because he is in charge,
because he is the first, because his father was a man who knew nothing more than to
drink and to destroy. But the smoke became his mother, became his father, became
a ceremony that became the thing that took the knife out of his heart.

II

It's 1953 and he and his father have just finished
with the hunt. He has shot a deer, his first, and he carries him home.

His hair is black, and shining with oil, his father walking next to him.
He knows what he has in his arms.

Tomorrow, he's going to go down to the junkyard, he's going to throw
his hands into the metal and garbage and come up with something structured.

This is the man whose guns brought him into the future, whose parts
were more than the sum of his whole, the child of those who used to kill men.

For my Uncle Harry, these days were like the days when he was married to his first
wife, the days that he would lean in and listen, and try to learn from a woman
who was not his mother, who was like his first deer, his arms carrying her home,
his father at his side, his guns and his future the same, his last, his first way home.

III

It's 1965. She's holding my cousins
in her arms, Ab's hand on her braid. She's just beginning to learn how to dance.

The powwow is filled with Indians who have just begun to grow
their braids. She has made her children their regalia and they bend their knees,

Straightdancing. Their tiny bodies are like hers, filled with the sound of drums.
Her hands are on the needle, no, not that one, the one that makes beadwork,

For strangers. And family. I hold a blue flower in my hands.
And even though they've stopped dancing, I know they can hear drums.

For my Auntie Edie, powwow was God, filling her with sound, her hands on the fan,
dancing traditional women's, her hands on her children, showing them how to dance,
her hands in the air, reaching for God, for her husband, who understands how her hands
in the air, on the fan, on her children, on me and my one blue flower are reaching for
the one true drum.

IV

It's 1966, and a man is leaning on her shoulder, kicking up
and she's looking into his face, his mask a mask.

Everyone's in costume, she is Pocahontas,
her dark face lighting up with the joke.

It's Texas, and beautiful, the desert stretching out like a cat
towards the sun, the sun like her mother now, missing her.

She dances and teaches school, her arms poetic, the children know
what they're seeing. This is the child of Apache gangsters, Chickasaw traditionalists.

For my mother, those days were like the days of her childhood,
leaning in, she and her siblings rapt, listening to the radio,
eyes closed & the volume up, everything like the cat, like the desert, like the cat
stretching into the desert, stretching into me.

V

It's 1985 and I am twelve years old. I am in a hotel room in New York and she is touching my father. I cry in the bathroom. She is the one

Whose mother ran away. Whose father was a man born from a man who drank, gambled and hit my grandmother. Whose father was not her father.

When she goes to live with my grandmother, she takes the food that they give her and runs to the corner, desperate. She is like an animal when they come near. Who

Touched her? This woman who loved everyone too much, who smelled like cigarettes, who I feared and wanted to love, who has children that I don't want to think about.

She is my aunt, my cousin, a woman I share no real blood with, a woman always reminding me of who my father really was. For her, every cigarette was the one that was going to fix everything, every touch was going to heal, to take the pain away. She is the one who has gone before everyone, fading away, like pollen in the wind.

MIRACLES DURING EVERY COMMERCIAL BREAK

Four dark heads surround the television screen, watching the 1957 American Beauty Pageant. Their little brown eyes are wide and beautiful and reflect everything. Their mother's arms encircle them. So does the glow from the television/vision. But they watch carefully. They wait for miracles during every commercial break.

It is that one woman, her arms wide, amongst her children with a revolution in her heart, sitting in an old leather chair, waiting for metaphor to change everything.

INDIAN FISH

All the Ocean before us, and Grandma inside
on the cracked brown leather chair, ready to catch us,
like the funny brown fish that we were,
straight from the Gulf of Mexico.

We would never drown.

Ab pushed Emily's head into the water
over and over, his long black-brown hands beautiful.
We called him little bear, cause of that curly brown hair.
I was miss 'merica. Ab couldn't say my name.

And Ty was just Ty
with the beautiful brown eyes
and hair like Crazyhorse's, but tied back,
his brain like polished silver.

Emily was the one who didn't sit at the table.
We'd laugh, and Emily would cry
and hit us when no one was around
and pray for brown eyes.

Grandma knew, we called her Mimi,
her arms like a ballet dancer's, balancing
on the ocean, her grandchildren swimming in her waters,
little fish, always trying to swim home.

OH, COUSIN

How we rode on your motorcycle that summer and every summer,
on those back roads behind my house,
the smell of the raspberry bushes after the rain everywhere.

I buried my mixed blood hands in your mixed blood hair, cut it, you said
and make it look like yours, but darker.
And I couldn't though I loved you more than anyone else.

How we laughed all night, tormenting
my brilliant younger sister who would grow up so angry and sad
just like dad, just like your dad too, both of them.

Oh, Ab, we grew up and got off that bike too quick,
you with babies and fists, and me, with words and nothing else.

Oh, Ab, let's get back on the bike, and stop, and pick those raspberries and make something
beautiful out of them and let's take my sister along this time, I miss her so much.

AT THE SPEED OF LIFE

It was that same drum that my cousin fancydanced to when he was just eight years old, before he collided with the world at the technologically advanced speed of light, that he touched with reverence when he was barely old enough to breathe.

Watch him, watch him make a portrait of his average Indian life. He's growing up with laughter and frybread and straightdancing with mom's homemade roach on his head and a Chickasaw girl's eyes moving in time but when that man put his hands on my cousin's tiny body, all it took was one moment to learn about the absolute power of destruction.

And now, with that man's hands still half on my cousin and my cousin's hands still half on the drum, that same drum, the one you and he dream about, he sits with the diabetic's needle in his hand on a good day after a day of living three jobs and four kids and one wife and 10,000 dreams beating in his heart on a good day on a day it didn't rain and on a day he didn't dream on a day that he learned again, again, about his hands and about the absolute power of destruction.

AS A RUBY

—for K. W.

She was tiny, precise and beautiful as a ruby, my sister,
the baby, her eyes shaped like almonds, her hands on the wheel, hip hop blasting
from the radio, driving somewhere on I-70 with those boys in the back, who knows
what they wanted, of her.

But she was mine, I remember that, with those eyes just like grandma's, pulling me
down to the ground and into the sky the next minute, her lips on the joint, her hands
in another girl's hair, tearing, and then, so gentle, waiting for her boyfriend to come
home.

Expecting and expectant, she wanted it all, and deserved it, her wild arms reaching
for everything, and coming home, empty as the tank of gas in her car, always almost
breaking down, but making it home, just in time to catch that last Indian train out of
town.

IN ORDER TO SAVE THE WOMAN

I've been told a million times that I've got to kill the Apache in order to save the woman and if I would love blindly love blind I would see the beauty of white hands, the beauty of white hands on me, I would feel them everywhere, especially inside but I like the look of brown eyes too much to enjoy the death and besides it's already begun, my skin yellow and my mind empty of the words that my grandmother used to explain exactly how she felt the first time she walked into the kitchen and the whole room was empty of the holy words that had filled the room only moments before.

HOW THE ENTIRE MIDWEST WAS ADOPTED INTO A LAKOTA FAMILY

My family, they were the horse thieves,
the gamblers, the prostitutes, the pimps
the ones who survived, the ones who killed the witnesses to their crimes—
and were therefore never prosecuted.

Whites crossed the streets of Houston at night,
those Indians had knives.
Five foot three with guns at their sides.

Now, they are the train thieves,
the gangsters, the drug dealers,
and some carry guns in their minds.
Though the pimps have all gone to heaven
and the prostitutes have all come home.

TIME TO DANCE

I want our lives to be a fancydance, for every Indian to run straight into the imagination without stopping for a drink first. I want my entire family to say no to the 9-5, say no to midnight special, say no to the first indescribable cigarette, say no to the men and the women who steal dreams easier than they steal hearts, say no to the rest of the world, and to say *fuck you* to anybody that tells them that now is not the time to dance.

BODIES, RISING

Loving my family is like working for peanuts
my emotions like an elephant, insatiable, remembering
the ones who came before me, those Apaches who took donkeys into Mexico
to live in boxcars boxcars boxcars tequila in their hands and Zapata on their minds,
those Chickasaws who had $$$ from somewhere one day and one of the first cars
America had ever seen the next, and the next, nowhere to live and those Cherokees
working in the cities posing beautiful, ghostlike,
only a black shroud over their bodies, rising.

AS INNOCENT AS YOUR MOTHER, AND MINE

She is that small Indian girl who locks herself in the bathroom to sniff aerosol as innocent as my mother, and yours, who sat with her brother in the back of the truck when they were children and sniffed the fumes from the gasoline tank and laughed and laughed all the way across the back roads the dirt from the road lifting up and filling the air with all that blurry, glittering beauty, their eyes dancing, their brain cells swimming, swimming through the water underground their little voices lifting and daddy driving, taking all of them, even that girl who locked herself in the bathroom somewhere, somewhere none of them care where as long as the truck keeps going as long as daddy never takes his hands from the wheel, as long as the ride never ends, the cedar flute blowing.

Promises

Marin, under the streetlight, dancing by herself,
is singing the same song somewhere, I know. Is waiting
for a car to stop, a star to fall, someone to change her life.
—Sandra Cisneros

AT THE ROLLER RINK, MELISSA

At the roller rink, Melissa, you told me
how you would make him love you
how he already did, your old white skates clacking against the rim
your hair dyed blonde and mine, dyed blonde too, but darkening in the florescent lights.

Melissa, only now do I want to tell you how he was only a dark-eyed Indian boy
and I barely a woman when he made me love him,
how I've made up stories for him, and for all
of those boys, yours & mine, stories for me, and you.

Oh, Melissa, how you disappeared & reappeared on my answering machine like magic.
How I hid from your voice and from everyone's.

Do you still think of me as an Indian Princess?

Oh, Melissa, I've held your child and a million other children in these arms
their hair soft against my light brown arms
and I've told no one
no one.

Melissa, girl I'll never know again
tell me, where has that dark eyed boy gone
and what, do you know, of him?

WHAT I KNOW IS THE FIGHT

What I know is the fight
the feeling of steel in the mind
and the hollow tunnel of heart
already blown completely clean.

What I know are the neighborhoods
the small towns filled with disfigured dreams
and brains locked from birth.

What I know is the fight
the Indian hands and the white
the Mexican hands and the
thrill that passes through them
when they touch
and when they burn.

THREE OUT OF FOUR

As three out of the four beautiful Mexican boys in my high school beat each other with statistic fists in the marijuana parking lot I cried for all of our sins, my best friend and I watching, our Indian hearts filling with pain, my best friend's boyfriend laughing wildly like he had just broken through the gates of his own imagination and our light brown hands pressing to our purple lips in silent prayer in the middle of the endless dawn.

GENOCIDE FISTS

So many runaways, so many
running after something and, like magic
disappearing.

I never knew their names, held myself like a child,
waiting for it to end, like it was 1492 in my heart and 1860 in my mind.

I was always waiting for those fists, Indian and white,
the strained faces and torn jeans and t-shirts smelling like cigarette smoke.

They wore their anger like powwow blankets, warming them when nothing else could.
Their fists broke through incest like this and through the fire of violence, saving them,
saving me.

I ate lunch under the display case in winter,
in Spring, outside, the mountains standing in front of me like an illusion.

One runaway turned up, his body mangled and torn from running in the mountains, the
cougar shot later that week, all of us left wondering why him, why the cougar and what
exactly lived in the mountains above.

MAMA, DON'T LET YOUR QUARTERBREEDS GROW UP TO BE COWBOYS

There they are at the rodeo
their black mustaches gleaming
their hands resting on the restless flanks of the horses.

Like bullfighters, they know what to do.

So beautiful, these cowboys who aren't cowboys
boys I've known from a distance, their hands rough
and tender.

Their bodies are like the horses' bodies, wet and newly born
in the sun, and the dust and the heat, their arms exact, their legs
fancydancing, squaredancing, dancing in between.

It's all about that moment, that rope around the neck,
that flash of tail, that broken horse that breaks so that it can move
the way that makes the audience rise and hold their arms out in prayer.

They move, their muscles pulling tight, their arms wearing secrets
Crazyhorse tattoos under their shirts, filled with spirit, filled
with the knowledge of death, running always with the horses

Like children running through the fields
running their hands through the flowers, running
away.

SCHOOL PORTRAITS

I remember you Santee, down
from the Santee Sioux reservation, I remember you

And so does Misty, bad girl, stealing
a kiss from you in the Coast to Coast as you swept the floors, giving
it to her boyfriend the next day, who ran

His fingers cracked from cleaning solution down my leg
in the library, one hand on me, the other
holding his love poem for her.

I never told Misty about his fingers, his face
in the yearbook, staring hard into her eyes, those two Indian children already
memories, graffiti spray painted straight into the walls of the heart.

YOU MAKE A FIST LIKE THIS

You make a fist like this
with my Indian hands and her Indian hands and hers
you make it walking down the street
when the white girls in their brand new truck come suddenly around the corner
your fingers accelerate.

You make a fist like this
with my head against the headboard dreaming
of something like this dreaming
with your textbooks asleep in your lap the radio on the numbers and the words moving
quietly beyond.

You make a fist like this
with the muscle of your heart pumping blood but only carefully

You make a fist like this
with the music of your heart beating only one sharp song over and over

You make a fist like this
with your heart building bridges that only lead back in

You make a fist like this
you make it
with your heart.

COLFAX RESERVATION TELEVISION

In this city
love comes cheap
and in a bag

sometimes

Running down streets
these cousins of mine
move backwards into that awkward fancydance

searching for something, these

Boys by the lake, the mountains behind them,
playing basketball
their restless Indian bodies
light and dark brown
offering
the homesick Hidatsa a beer
while the baby cries for Ute daddy
but he's in jail for, shhh, don't talk about it
the baby's sleeping in the next room

but her daddy's been watching

The TV, the screen staring back
the bars reaching
around the lake

they can stop you

from drowning.

PRESSING MATTRESSES TO WALLS

—for M. White & her grandma

She was the one with the bowl in her hands watching
John Wayne watching her moving up the line.

She was the one who had dropped the bowl in front of the camera and
the one who had been waiting outside the drugstore with the other Indians waiting
for the producers who had been shopping for Indians and
she was the one for sale.

She was the woman who had pressed mattresses to walls with hands thickened
by life head moving against the tide face old and tired and she was the one
pressing mattresses to walls in the unsung ghetto apartment in the middle of Denver.

She was the one fearing bullets and ghosts pressing mattresses and hands
who fled into the darkness only knowing one thing after all of that time
that the bowl and the mattresses had become the same sin as the sins
that had never been sung before.

CANNOT BE MOVED WEST
—for M. White

I'd been driving forever in my old orange bronco
every moment knowing that I could break down
every moment now buried in those old checkered seats.

She'd sat beside me for years in that car, living in that trailer, her mother talking story
with her GPC cigarettes in her old Apache/Cherokee hands, the apple tree in back, Pink Floyd
in the tape deck, her hair thick and dark, an Indian promise but for what, I know the boys
who loved her never knew.

We drove past the same baseball field again and again in Idaho Springs, until the cops
were called. We drove though the fields in Denver and always got stuck. We drove to
every boyfriend she ever had and we are still in that car, I know it.

Misty, how I want that final destination, that tiny space inside the heart, that tiny bit
of unmovable love that thing that cannot be touched cannot be moved West.

OLD FURNITURE AND VISIONS

The middle-aged Ute is selling old furniture and visions on Colfax again. He smiles and shakes our brown hands—loosely—he ain't surprised that out of all the garage sales we could've come to, we ended up at his. He's got exactly what we need, and we push everything into the back of my truck.

The truck stalls
I
put my head in my hands
Yvonne
waits for it to end
We
try the car again
and she moves down the road like a vanished nightmare into the raw and purple dawn.

HANDS RESTING
—for Y. J. & Marshall

At the grocery store
in the middle of the Southwest,
she held his hands, her own
clasped in prayer over his, her mind
clasped in prayer, over his.

He, looking so much like his father,
who disappeared and never came back.
Dad, White Mountain, and she,
looking so much like his mother.
Mom, Navajo, who always threw him out
whenever there was a new man.

As the bum held out the bottle of windex,
his hands folding outwards, and drinking deeply
and holding the bottle of blue like an offering,
her hands moved rapidly to her chest,
her heart beat wildly.

Later, his eyes on hers,
in her bed, shaking wildly in sickness,
his black black hair falling all over his body
and reflecting no light, everything was
religious, the peyote working the only magic it could.

And years later,
driving around Farmington,
her hands on the wheel
her eyes roving over the red red landscape,
waiting for that black black hair to appear on the horizon
like god
so that both of their hands could finally fold outwards,
and rest.

BLUES, BEAUTY AND INDIAN CIGARETTES

—for Y. J.

She pulled back her sleeves revealing long textured lines. Almost like velvet, these lines, and she pulls her fingers over them with love.

These lines she loves, these lines that run so close to her heart, they tell me about midnight in the bathroom alone, waiting by the sink, wrists hanging lonely over the edge.

They tell me about her mother who shook violently on the bed, the needles pouring into her arms like rain, speaking in Navajo and in English, always mother, who then, without warning, simply floated away.

They tell me about the boys she chased with dirt in their hands and knives in their hearts and about the one who didn't get away, wish he had gotten away, they tell me about the man living in the distance, the one with the funny hands who held and held and never let go.

They tell me about awake and dreaming in the afterglow after he had gone and the wanting more and the leaning into the wind so that maybe she could reach it.

Oh how she spoke the beautyway when she lit her cigarette, smoke curling around the edges of her words.

GREEN TRUCK

—for Y. J.

This man I knew, a skinny old man who smiled and sat in front of the television, the light playing out on his face and his cane in his hand, a man who loved his daughter more than anything, this man died with tears in his eyes, with a small sigh of relief in a plain white hospital bed, in the middle of the Indian Southwest.

She said he gave her everything, a new green truck, her mother, her lover and her own heart.

And god you took her mother and the car was repossessed and her lover wanders slowly through the desert longing for his own heart but I know I know I know how much he loved her I know what love is I know everything in this moment I know . . .

WHAT ABOUT JACKIE?

But what about Jackie?
She drove miles and miles to get to the IHS clinic in Ignacio on time,
only to find the doors closed and the doctors sitting behind women
with white and pink hairclips nestled into black hair moving straight into the night.

She said she knew his name once
she said she knew all of their names
she said she had all of them in her book
she said she used to write in that book everyday, just a few thoughts, just a few names.

She said he had a safe brown face and long brown fingers (crooked) that he used
to make everything ok.
She said there had been a fat black clock on the dresser, there was always a clock on the dresser
and that it had spoken to her in loud red colors until

Jackie, like a ghost, like a machine, like a ghost in my machine
told me so many things before she disappeared into the night, into my heart, Jackie.

WALKING HOME

Walking home in Durango, a prayer in the middle of the night, waiting silently for the dawn. We were so young, and that dawn, it never came. And those Mexican boys, eyes Mayan and so beautiful, picking tiger lilies for us and laughing, our Indian fingers reaching for the petals, and finding the rain, we were so young, and that dawn, it never came.

LEAVING DURANGO

And in this valley next to thunderbolt-split trees and rivers,
the light of this city flooding the plains and sitting silently in the foothills,
I stagger in through the distance and wait for the bus to pull in,
the dust from the old seats filling the lungs of all the others on this silver bus,
knowing that I'll remember everything about your hands,
the memory moving through the air and filling the other Skins on the bus with electricity.
It hurts almost as much as where the Ute fell asleep on my shoulder,
her dreams mingling with the sweat-stained cushions, a moment of tribal reconciliation
but she doesn't know what I've done with you by the side of a mountain,
your white hands coursing down my body like water traveling home.

Indian Trains

. . . we were drinking whiskey, whispering, trading
secrets in the gloom, twenty Indin kids on the edge
of the desert Looking for the easy way out Looking
for the ocean where it don't hardly rain.

—Diane Burns

INSIDE BOTH OF US

. . . the sheep were like the dead like his eyes on the pearl street mall and he said he brought the rain down from pine ridge why couldn't he bring it down in arizona why can't he bring it down inside both of us moving quickly towards the burning bush towards the cracked and bloody desert the weavers bringing the rain down the bums bringing the rain down why can't I bring the rain down he said hey sister got a dollar sister got a home for me sister we natives gotta stick together just one more dollar will keep me warm all night its ok that I put my hand on your long brown shoulder put your hand on my long brown heart so the sheep will rise again so the water will turn to wine and back to water and bring the rain down inside both of us . . .

CLOSER

. . . Ah Samuel with your Jesus eyes how you looked at me that day on the hill by the school with your hands in the air praying in Navajo and Chippewa for more how you asked for my name for my tribe and for my phone number saying sister sister sister how I love your hair sister how I love the black of it sister come a little closer here put this coconut oil in your hair and make it grow so long so long its promise will cover the world twice over how much I've learned out here how much I still want to know and someday I'll call you and tell you when I've finished knowing and speak to you of all of my secrets ah Samuel how I saw you weeks later farther down that newly blackened road giving all of your secrets to that lanky white Boulder boy, but you had said on that day on the hill you know the Navajo are a shy people don't be shy come here and hold me hold me sister so deep inside . . .

YOU DIDN'T WANT A DOLLAR, YOU WANTED ME

Ah Gerald you didn't want a dollar you wanted me by the side of the school in the heat
with all of the children just past childhood milling, milling, waiting Gerald for you and
for me in the heat just waiting for you to tell me about how you didn't drink but that you
were thirsty, Gerald so thirsty in this heat & did I know where we could get a drink, just
one because you didn't drink, you never drink but did I Oh Gerald how you beat your
wheelchair and one leg with both fists how you ran your hands down the length of all of
your scars, purple as the sunset in the dying, dying day those Sundance scars those
surgery scars the war scars oh you told me didn't you Gerald that you were a vet of one
war and three wives who had all wanted you to stay home but you were a warrior sister
you said I'm ugly but I've gotten a lot of beautiful Indian women do you mind if I call
you beautiful no Gerald no but Gerald when I asked you when was the last time that
you'd been home you said thirty years and that you'd never go home again you said there
ain't nothin to do there but ride horses but Jesus Gerald you have nothing but one leg and
four exes but I think that you could still ride horses I really think that you could and
maybe they've been waiting for you to come home, the brown and the black and the paint
have been waiting for you to come home and ride them one last time, ride them past all
you've ever known.

THE NEEDLE IN THE BOX

That year you lived in the house with the white girl who never stopped asking you inside who never stopped asking you to come and hold her who one day told you that she knew that you were the devil and the next an angel, God, that year you watched the Lakotas watch the Jazz musician shoot up before he played from your window your lonely Navajo eyes filing with desolate visions oh that year that year was the year you decided that you'd never be alone that you'd call everyone in your family that you'd drive all night if you had to you'd phone from every pay phone West you'd get a girlfriend and watch me from the box and that year was the year you found out more than you ever wanted and more than you ever got.

ON THE BUS, ON THE BENCH
—for C. N.

On the bus, on the bus, on the bus coming home she saw them on the bench laughing,
laughing at the man whose beautiful Cree face could be her own, could be her father's,
and stumbling on his way home, the whiskey burning deep and clean into his stomach
so that each day could pass like a beautiful dream,
She jumped off that bus and told those children not to laugh.

On the bench, on the bench, on the bench she sat with all of her white friends,
laughing at something, not even seeing the beautiful Cree face that could be her own,
her father's, stumbling, the whiskey burning deep and clean into his stomach
so that each day could pass like a beautiful dream.
She told that woman that she was not laughing.

Sister, sister that woman said, I'm sorry I didn't know, don't you know, you have to
protect your own, don't you know the dreams that he carries in his heart, in his brown
bag, in mine, in yours on the bus, on the bench, on the bus, sister don't you know your
own heart?

ON THE ROOFTOP

And on the rooftop
I find you
in the twilight downtown
broken
passed out
after the best damn '49 in history.

Tracks

I did not understand his doom or my taste for the big dangerous body . . . he was souped-up and stunned and cruel. He taught me to love what was stuck, what couldn't help itself, what went down mute into time, like tar, like anger.

—Sharon Olds

PISTONS

Go West, Young Man

My father has traveled years for this. He has pushed the frontier of himself to complete the already completed American story. He will fight for the American dream. Win against the American dollar. He will watch the Denver skies and count himself among the lucky.

Western Wear

In the fifties my mother learned how to dance and her sister learned how to powwow.

The Wild Wild West Show

My father is dreaming
& the darkness is complete
& has nothing to do with my mother's hair

and as a little Indian girl I watched his fists move up and down like the pistons on a train.

IRON INSECT

He lit it on fire
and it backed out
that summer day
with his white hands
resting gently under my brown eyes
with his white hands
holding my iron tears

HOW TO FINANCE AN ILLUSION

If eyes are windows to the soul, the house is empty and dad's drunk again.

In the basement of my mind he stands, white hands shaking and blood vessels breaking, memory lapsing like a tidal wave.

His family sits in the living room, waiting for just enough money to finance our illusions.

If we can slip through the days we can find a way to rent that tiny apartment in town. It's ugly but it's heaven for three Indian women who have had enough of alcohol soaking into their dreams.

We sleep on mattresses on the floor, mom staring in wonder at the open refrigerator door and my sister and I staring with wonder at the empty walls.

Mom would phone home but dad and mom are gone, one from the gun and the other from the gun.

Aunts and Uncles flood the streets like an Indian parade an AIM weekend getaway but nobody can talk her into coming home. They want to move every ratty piece of furniture into the Texas sunrise.

Mom prays every night even though she don't believe in god anymore and waits for our whispering to stop before she turns out the light and goes to sleep. She knows she'll be counting her change in bed and that we'll be dreaming of him.

Finally, when the phone stops ringing, mom will put her second hand copy of *Co-Dependent No More* down. And pick the receiver up. And pull her head into her hands, speaking, as if for the first time.

OLD GUITAR AND ALCOHOL

Your Indian daughter loves you more than ever before dad
Picking up where you left off . . .
old guitar and alcohol.

I hold this instrument in the exact way
I held you
awkwardly, and with love.

LAST INDIAN TRAIN

And on that last Indian train I thought I was being pulled straight
towards your grave again, straight towards that swollen, angry ground and as
it pulled and strained and groaned underground my insides giving birth I thought
of what you'd always said about Indian trains and about Indians dad you said you didn't
know what track they were leaving from or what their destination was dad neither do I

SAVAGE SKIN

—for M. W.

My hands were like angels
holding the phone that day that you called
asking if I'd seen the sunset
sitting amongst all of those nature poets talking politics.

M, you knew that I was watching, you knew as you knew everything,
your voice like a ghost,
like a dead relative whose body I should not see in the traditional way.

M, how you ran and how you died inside
and how much I wanted to see you flower
and love your own beautiful skin, how you touched mine
and listened to those family stories, my apartment filled with the smell
of sweetgrass and the smell of your sweet Indian skin.

LEAVING THE GARDEN WILD

—for M. W.

In Colorado, my love, it has rained for 40 days and 40 nights,
the water running in the streets like an ocean, rushing down the sidewalks, lost,
completely lost.

Even the weather here has biblical ramifications.

When you left, the sun trailed after you, behind the flatirons,
though I didn't know it at the time.
Now I see that was one of your many secrets.

In my old apartment, the floors covered in wood, sweetgrass still hanging in the air,
the walls blank now that I am gone too, you touched me
for the first time, your hands burning like the desert sun into my hair.

Here too, innocence was lost.

DANCING BACKWARDS

—for M. W.

Watching the clock tick backwards in the mirror alone
I move in the same direction
every Indian does it
but I begin to wonder why I ever left home and
why I lied to you that summer in Boulder when you came back to me—
god we were hot and dancing backwards.

SUFFERING FROM POST-POWWOW DEPRESSION

This year, I let the lightbulbs go out
one by one
until there was darkness.

Sometimes the light
of the television
would come alive
and keep me company.

I'm not sure
how many Indians
live
just like this.

CUT THE ROPE

Cut the rope he said, cut the rope
all it takes is long Indian hair
and a graveyard of old fords
and a condom thrown onto the wooden floor.

Cut the rope he said, cut the rope
do it with his hands and his hands and mine
and all of those words trapped inside.

Cut the rope he said, cut the rope.

Dad your hands were white and M your hands are brown
they are the same hands
but I have the knife I have the knife I have to

Cut the rope, he said, cut it and you will find . . .

GOING BACK

I went back, I went back
I haunted your shell
And your hands, they were just like his.

I like that destruction
Sweet, it makes my teeth ache.

It was just like in my childhood memories, remember?
Five white girls with minds like furnaces came at me with hands like . . .
And they bit in to my Indian skin, and it felt good. It was just Punishment.

When they take me away, I want their hands to be just like yours, long, I want their hands
to be just like the first dark eyed boy's, long, I want their hands to be just like yours,
strange, just like dad's too. When they take me away, and I am sentenced to sit inside
myself, and all I have is time and you, I want all of their hands to rest.

TRAINS IN THE DISTANCE

the train the train the train
I've always lived by an Indian train
and although you said you wanted all of me in Iowa City
I can still hear that long low whistle in the distance.